Chilham Railway Station

Circular Walks

1. From the Bottom to the Top
2. One for the Tree Lovers
3. Around the lake
4. The Down Walk

● Start/end of walk

Introduction

The village of Chilham is one of the most attractive in the county of Kent. The historic square and the small roads leading to it have a number of timber and plaster, and weather worn brick houses. The mansion which lies adjacent to the village was built between 1603 and 1616 and was designed by Inigo Jones, whilst the grounds were created by John Tradescant in the 1620s and Capability Brown in the 1780s. Parklands are a feature of this part of the Stour Valley and two of the walks pass through Godmersham Park.

The only remaining evidence of hop gardens are the oast houses converted to private dwellings. However, there are still many orchards providing the 'Garden of England' landscape.

As elsewhere in the Stour Valley, gravel has been dug at Chilham and this has resulted in a very attractive series of lakes, which have been made accessible to the public by Mid-Kent Water.

Downland on either side of the Stour Valley is still valuable for wildlife, and conservation organisations and some local landowners are attempting to reverse the decline of chalk grassland habitat in the area.

On the plateaus above Chilham are some outstanding areas of woodland; King's Wood to the west and Denge Wood to the east. These ancient woodlands consist of sweet chestnut coppice, modern conifer and beech plantations, occasional stands of ash and hornbeam as well as magnificent individual trees.

Most of the walks are in the Kent Downs Area of Outstanding Natural Beauty.

The district is crossed by two recreational routes - the North Downs Way and the Stour Valley Walk and two of the trails take advantage of these well-used rights of way, but for much of the time the trails follow lesser known paths that show the full beauty and range of this part of Kent.

Acknowledgments
English Nature
Kent County Council
Kent Wildlife Trust
Selling Parish Council
Sunley Farms Limited

Chilham est l'un des villages les plus attractifs de la région du Kent. Sa place historique et les ruelles qui y conduisent recèlent de nombreuses maisons en colombage ainsi que des maisons en briques rongées par les intempéries. L'hôtel particulier attenant au village, conçu par Inigo Jones, fut construit entre 1603 et 1616; les jardins furent dessinés dans les années 1620 par John Tradescant, et repensés par Capability Brown dans les années 1780. De plus, de nombreux parcs agrémentent cette partie de la vallée de la Stour, et deux des balades proposées ici traversent Godmersham Park, ou Parc de Godmersham.

Les dernières traces de la présence de houblonnières sont aujourd'hui uniquement visibles au niveau des séchoirs à houblon reconvertis en demeures privées. Par contre, on rencontre encore de nombreux vergers qui caractérisent ce paysage régional dit du "Jardin de l'Angleterre".

Comme partout dans la vallée de la Stour, cette région a été sujette à l'extraction de graviers, ce qui résulte à Chilham en une série de lacs accessibles au public.

Les collines des Downs entourant la vallée de la Stour conservent un grand intérêt pour la nature. Organisations de conservation de la nature ainsi que propriétaires fonciers locaux s'efforcent ainsi d'inverser le déclin des pelouses crayeuses.

Le plateau surplombant Chilham supporte quant à lui d'éminents vieux bois : King's Wood à l'Ouest, et Denge Wood à l'Est. Essentiellement taillis de châtaigniers, ils comportent également des plantations d'hêtres et de conifères, d'occasionnels frênes et charmes, ainsi que quelques magnifiques et imposants arbres isolés.

La plupart des balades de cette brochure se situent par ailleurs dans la zone des Kent Downs classée pour sa beauté naturelle (Area of Outstanding Natural Beauty).

Enfin, la contrée est traversée par les itinéraires de randonnée bien fréquentés du North Downs Way et du Stour Valley Walk, qu'empruntent en partie deux des balades proposées ici. Les circuits suivent cependant la plupart du temps des sentiers moins connus depuis lesquels l'on peut apprécier en toute quiétude la beauté de cette partie du Kent.

1. From the Bottom to the Top

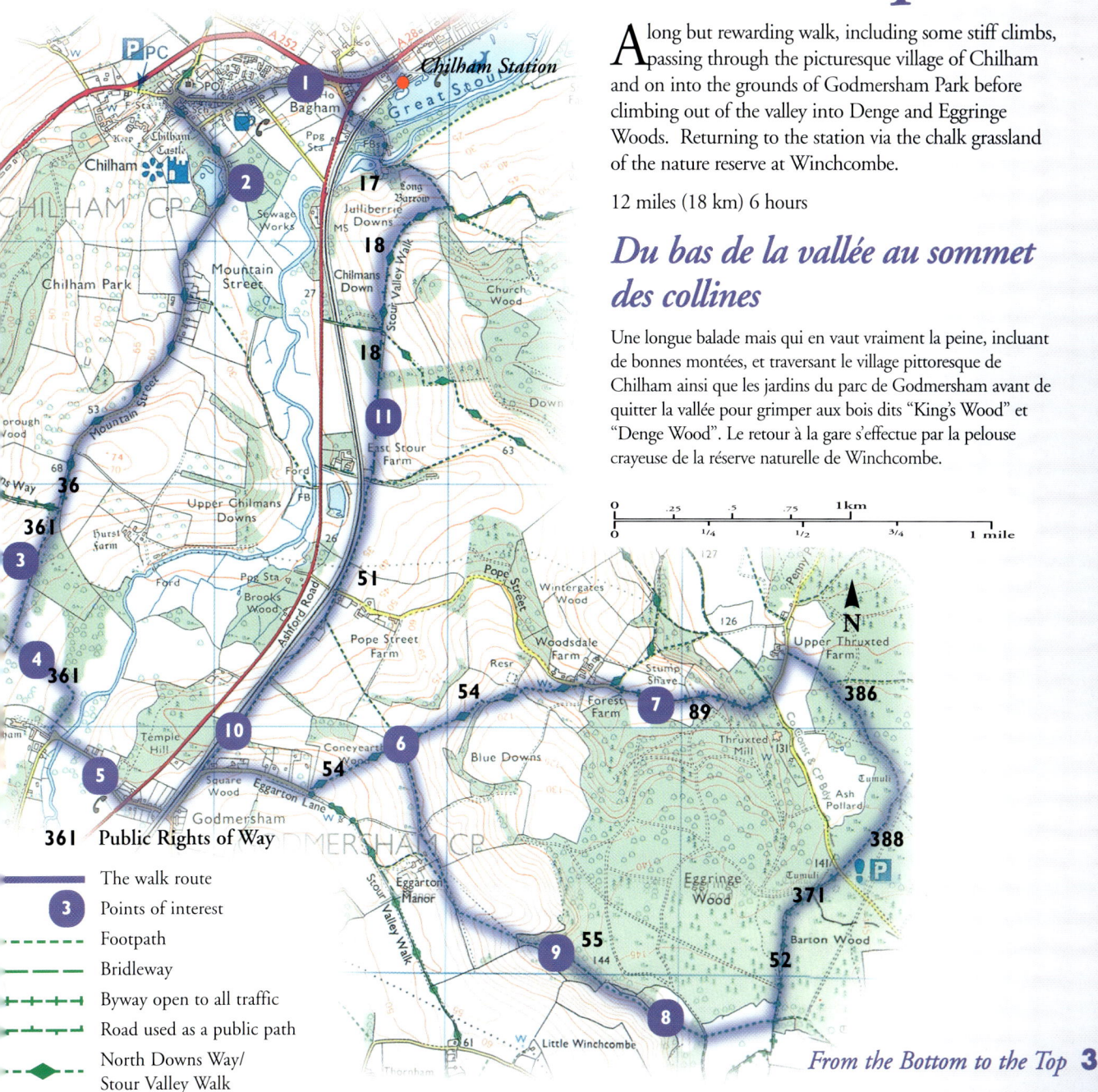

A long but rewarding walk, including some stiff climbs, passing through the picturesque village of Chilham and on into the grounds of Godmersham Park before climbing out of the valley into Denge and Eggringe Woods. Returning to the station via the chalk grassland of the nature reserve at Winchcombe.

12 miles (18 km) 6 hours

Du bas de la vallée au sommet des collines

Une longue balade mais qui en vaut vraiment la peine, incluant de bonnes montées, et traversant le village pittoresque de Chilham ainsi que les jardins du parc de Godmersham avant de quitter la vallée pour grimper aux bois dits "King's Wood" et "Denge Wood". Le retour à la gare s'effectue par la pelouse crayeuse de la réserve naturelle de Winchcombe.

361 Public Rights of Way

- The walk route
- **3** Points of interest
- Footpath
- Bridleway
- Byway open to all traffic
- Road used as a public path
- North Downs Way/Stour Valley Walk

From the Bottom to the Top **3**

On reaching the main road turn left. Take the right hand fork (A259) in the road, taking care when crossing the road (A28). After a short distance take the road to the left and then right up to the village of Chilham.

Lining the road is an avenue of common limes (Tilia x vulgaris) 1 . This tree is a hybrid of the native small-leaved and large-leaved lime (T. cordata and platyphyllos) and has been widely planted becoming very much part of the landscape whilst its parents are almost forgotten. Pollen records show that small-leaved lime was once one of the most common trees of the "wildwood", but now it is difficult to find growing wild. It hangs on in the remnants of ancient woods and in hedges that are the "ghosts" of cleared forests. This tree had a number of uses in the past. There is a fibrous layer between the bark and the sapwood that was stripped for what was called "bast" which was twisted into rope. Its timber was also prized for wood carving and was the material favoured by the famous wood carver Grinling Gibbons, some of whose work can be seen in St. Paul's Church, Covent Garden where an intricate frieze depicts a wreath of flowers and fruit, some with stalks only a fraction of an inch thick.

On reaching the Woolpack Inn bear right up The Street.

On the right is St. Mary's Church most of which dates from the fifteenth century although there are building records from 1280 and it was recorded in the 1085 Domesday Book. Its interior was much restored in the Victorian period. The church contains a number of monuments and stained glass windows commemorating families associated with the village. In the north aisle there is a polished Bethersden marble memorial to Sir Dudley Digges, who owned Chilham Castle in the early seventeenth century. In the north chapel a memorial to the two Hardy children who died in 1858 depicts them, with their toys around them, reading "The Babes in the Wood". The Hardy family is also commemorated in the stained glass of the north and south windows. At the eastern end of the chancel a large Purbeck marble sarcophagus is said to have held the bones of Thomas á Becket when they were moved there in 1535 to escape the ravages of Henry VIII. It has been calculated that the yew tree (Taxus baccata), between the war memorial and the church entrance, would have been planted about 690 AD. Half of it was removed in 1792 so that the villagers could see the church clock; it was also damaged in the 1987 hurricane but still lives on.

On reaching The Square it is easy to see why the village of Chilham is one of the most visited in Kent, the gates to Chilham Castle at one end the church at the other, and a cluster of timber and plaster and weather worn brickwork houses around The Square; the village pre-dates these Tudor and Jacobean houses by many centuries. Its written history dates back to the second Roman invasion when the downs above the village were possibly the site of one of the first major battles between the Romans and the Britons.

As with most villages, Chilham has its share of ghosts, secrets and intrigues. On stormy nights the ghost of a hooded monk, complete with flickering candle, is said to frequent the churchyard where he meets a skeletal horse, then they both disappear through a door in the churchyard wall. The Woolpack Inn, which has its own ghost of a grey lady, has a long standing tradition that it has a tunnel big enough to for a coach and horses to be driven through running from its cellar to Chilham Castle. There are a number of theories as to why the tunnel existed. One was that it was used to transport ale for banquets at the castle; another is the that the inn is alleged to have been a courthouse and prisoners were brought from the castle to be tried there. In 1994, in an attempt to lay the matter to rest, the pub manager and some locals set out to discover what was behind the thick cellar wall. What they found was large and ancient, but unfortunately it was a large and ancient drain.

Chilham centre

From the Bottom to the Top

Leave The Square via School Hill to the left of the castle gates. At the T-junction turn right into Mountain Street.

It is possible to find growing on and at the base of the large brick wall [2] that bounds the castle's grounds, two plants that were once important herbal medicines. The first is pellitory-of-the-wall (Parietaria judaica) which can be found growing directly out of the mortar between the bricks. Because it grew on stone it was thought to be a cure for kidney and bladder stones. The other is common comfrey (Symphytum officanale) whose credentials as a herbal cure are much more proven. It was, and still is, used to make a very effective poultice for sprains, bruises and abrasions as it contains allantoin which has been scientifically proven to promote the healing of connective tissue. Its often used alternative name is knitbone as its roots were once harvested and grated up and then used on broken bones in a similar manner as plaster of Paris is today.

As the road bears left go straight on through the small gate onto B36. Pass through the next small gate and carry straight on, now FP 361, into Godmersham Park.

The Godmersham estate now covers 860 acres (345 hectares) although it was once much

Godmersham House

bigger. It is one of the finest examples of a Kentish landscape with its parkland, river meadows, woodland and chalk grassland. The Manor of Godmersham dates back many centuries. It was first recorded in a charter in 824 AD when Archbishop Wulfred was given the manor by Beornulph, King of Mercia and again in the Anglo-Saxon Charter of 1036 when Archbishop Athelnoth granted it to the Monks of Christ Church, Canterbury. It remained in the church's possession until 1590 when the part of the manor that went on to be Godmersham Park was acquired by the Brodnax family. Thomas Brodnax built the mansion in 1732 on the site of a much older house called Ford Place. In 1812 the manor was inherited by Edward Austin-Knight, the brother of Jane Austin. Jane was a frequent visitor and it is alleged that she wrote some of her works here.

Godmersham Park and its inhabitants supposedly inspired "Mansfield Park" and Revd. Collins' vicarage in "Pride and Prejudice" was based on a building on the estate.

The Park's decline began in the 1870s until it was purchased by the present owner, Mr. John Sunley, in 1983. He has commenced an extensive restoration programme to bring the parkland back to its former glory. Hundreds of trees have been planted to replace the ageing parkland trees that survived the 1987 hurricane.

Pass over the stile next to the double gates.

The hedges alongside the horse paddocks [3] were planted under a scheme called Countryside Stewardship which provides monetary incentives to manage land for wildlife, landscape and people. This enlightened management by the estate's owner has proved to be the catalyst for a number of other farmers and estate managers in the area to enter parts of their holdings into the scheme.

On the right is Deer Lodge and, as the name suggests, it was the home of the Park's Deer Keeper, it is now a private house.

At the cross road of tracks turn left onto FP 361.

Looking back up the track evidence of our ancestors can be seen in the arable field to the left [4]. A system of terracing known as "lynchets" is very apparent in the field before the crop has grown but can clearly be seen at anytime of year as they continue across the track. They are medieval or perhaps earlier in origin and enabled the steep slope of the down to be cultivated a little more easily.

Go through the next gate and turn right. Head for another small gate opposite the brick gatehouse. Pass through it and turn immediately left through the iron gates onto the road. Carry on straight ahead over the bridge.

The bridge was built in 1698 on the site of a ford across the River Great Stour. Looking down stream a stone construction can be seen. This a fish weir, built by the estate to prevent the river bed silting

From the Bottom to the Top **5**

up. A gravelly river bed is essential for fish to spawn into. Although this was constructed to enhance the game fishing on this part of the river it does have immense value to other wildlife especially white-clawed crayfish (Austropotamobius pallipes). This crayfish is the country's only, and increasingly rare, species of freshwater crayfish and it needs a stony river bed. During the summer, the surface of the river is coated with mats of the white flowers of river water crowfoot (Ranunculus fluitans).

Looking up the bank on the left a white building in the style of a Greek temple 5 can be seen. This is one of Godmersham Park's follies. It is said that this is where Jane Austen liked to write. As well as the references to the area in her novels, she mentions her stays at the estate many times in various letters although, at times, she did seem a little lonely there. In one letter she says: "We dine at Chilham Castle tomorrow and I expect to find some amusement. I am all alone, Edward gone to the woods. At the present time I have five tables, eight and twenty chairs and two fires all to myself".

On reaching the main road cross straight over to the road opposite. After passing under the railway bridge turn left into Eggarton Lane. Follow the road until turning left over a stile onto FP 54. Go straight up over the arable field. At the cross road of tracks carry straight on up the rise and then pass over the next field in the same direction.

White-clawed crayfish

Volunteers from the Kentish Stour Countryside Project carrying out conservation work on the Godmersham estate

At the top of the bank, 6 looking back over the valley it is finally possible to see Chilham Castle. This site above the valley has been a strong point for thousands of years. There was certainly a hill fort there at the time of the previously mentioned battle. The victorious Romans possibly built a small fort on the site. As time went by the site's occupiers included the Saxon kings Hengist and Withred. At the time of the Norman Conquest it was owned by the Saxon thane Sired, who fought on the side of Harold at Hastings and consequently lost all his lands. After Hastings, it was one of the estates grabbed by Bishop Odo, the new Earl of Kent, who let it out to Fulbert de Lucy.

It was de Lucy who built the first wooden castle there after he was given the land, when Odo was banished for plotting against the king, on the condition that he provided troops to garrison Dover Castle. The octagonal stone keep seen today replaced the original wooden one in 1171.

From the Bottom to the Top

Chilham Castle

Although the castle was never directly fought over some of its owners met with untimely ends. Bartholomew of Badlesmere, who was granted the estate by Edward II in 1312, repaid his benefactor by joining the barons' rebellion against him. Unfortunately, he was captured and sent to Canterbury where he was hung, drawn and quartered. The castle and estate eventually came into the possession of Sir Dudley Digges who began work on the mansion in 1603. The house, designed by Inigo Jones, took 13 years to complete. The carefully tended grounds were created by two of this country's finest gardeners - John Tradescant in the 1620s and Capability Brown in the 1780s. Today both the keep and the mansion are private residences.

On reaching the trees turn left, then right shortly after. After passing through the trees turn left along them. Pass over the stile and cross diagonally right over the pasture to a stile to the right of the buildings. At the junction of tracks take the middle one following the Stour Valley Walk until it branches off to the left. Carry straight on, now B 89.

The path runs along the bottom of a V-shaped dry valley **7**, one of many that cut across the North Downs formed by rivers during the Ice Ages. Although the ice sheet ended just north of the Thames, the downs were a very cold place, similar to the Arctic tundra of today with an almost permanent covering of snow and ice, some of which would have melted each summer sending cascades of water down into the valleys.

Opposite the house turn left through the gate. Cross diagonally right across the pasture to another gate into the wood, then follow the track through it.

This wood is a fairly typical chalk woodland, with its beeches and yews (Fagus sylvatica and Taxus baccata). Growing under the larger trees are butcher's broom and wild privet (Ruscus aculeatus and Ligustrum vulgare). This is the country's native privet and was used widely for hedging before it was superseded by the much more well known garden privet (L. ovalifolium) after it was introduced from Japan. Our native privet has narrower leaves than the garden variety although both have the clusters of creamy-white flowers that develop into the familiar black berries. The berries are poisonous and can be fatal to children if eaten.

On reaching the road turn left then, opposite Upper Thruxted Farm, turn right onto FP 386. Cross straight over the arable field and enter the wood.

The trail now passes through a complex of woods which is collectively known as Denge Wood. This large series of woods has mostly been converted to sweet chestnut coppice (Castanea sativa) or conifer plantation, and is actively managed for its timber, although some relict native woodland has survived. Because of its large size and the wide range of soil types, it is still a very diverse and important forest for both flora and fauna. The heavy clay soil of the plateau is dominated by bluebells and wood anemones (Endymion non-scriptus and Anemone nemorosa) while the chalky dry valleys are ideal for orchids such as the lady, greater and lesser butterfly (Orchis purpurea, Platanthera chlorantha and latifolia).

Take the right-hand fork in the path, FP 388. On reaching the track turn right. At the next junction of tracks turn right, sign-posted "car park". On reaching the car park carry on to the road and cross over to the track opposite, for a short distance B 371 then B 52.

As is often the case with these plantation woodlands on top of the downs, it is along the edge of the tracks that the greatest profusion of wildlife can be found as they are open to the sun. Along these sunny rides plants such as black knapweed, tufted vetch and trailing tormentil (Centaurea nigra, Vicia cracca and Potentilla anglica) can be found. The knapweed is a plant that produces lots of nectar and therefore is very attractive to butterflies which, in high summer, can be found here in huge numbers. Other

From the Bottom to the Top **7**

possibilities are species of day-flying moth. During late spring and early summer, speckled yellow (Pseudopanthera macularia) is almost guaranteed and is quite easy to identify as it is speckled and yellow! Later in the summer the migratory silver Y (Autographa gamma) is a possibility. Again they are fairly east to identify if for no other reason than that they are about the only brown moth active in day-light, and a close look will reveal the presence of a silver Y on the top wing.

Speckled yellow moth

On reaching a fork in the track, go left. At the next, again go left. Just after the track leaves the trees turn right onto FP 55 or for food and drink continue on to the village of Sole Street and The Compasses Inn. Cross the arable field bearing left to a stile through the hedge. Cross over the track to another stile then bear right. Follow the fence line on the left to another stile, cross over it and follow the path along the top of the bank.

Carline thistle

The field crossed and this bank 8 are part of a Site of Special Scientific Interest. Its importance is in its plant and butterfly communities that are associated with this type of chalk grassland. One of the characteristic plants is the carline thistle (Carlina vulgaris). Its odd looking flower looks dead, even when it is newly formed and is surrounded by long, shiny yellow bracts that open in warm, dry weather and close when it is cool and damp. In spite of its dull appearance it is very popular with butterflies that find it as attractive as its more showy relations.

Pass through the small band of scrub and continue along the bank, then pass over the stile into the wood.

Growing in some profusion in this wood 9 is stinking iris (Iris foetidissima). Another name for this native is roast-beef plant as the leaves, if rubbed, smell of stale, raw beef. Although its flowers are a little modest, being pale blue or purple with a faint network of darker lines, its seeds are striking. When the large pods split in the autumn they reveal rows of bright orange seeds. Because of this splash of late colour it has become a popular garden plant, but here it can still be found growing wild.

Exit the wood and bear right over the arable field. Pass through the paddocks using the stiles then cross over the track and follow the left-hand edge of the field. At the cross road of paths turn left down the bank, FP 54, and re-trace the trail to the lane and turn right. As Eggarton Lane turns left to follow the railway, turn right over a stile and follow the fence line, FP 51.

At the top of this field is a massive sweet chestnut (Castanea sativa) 10. A mature sweet

Stinking iris

From the Bottom to the Top

Chilham Mill

chestnut is very different from the more often encountered coppiced form. The huge trunk with its spiral of deep fissures is the root of one of this trees alternative names, Spanish dancer, as the twist in the bark supposedly resembles the swirl of a flamenco dancer's skirt The Romans have been wrongly credited with many additions to this country's wildlife, but on this occasion it was they who introduced this species. Its nuts were ground into flour by the legionnaires. It now considered to be an "honorary native" and in this part of the country it does behave like one - being well-established in ancient woodlands and able to propagate itself. There are a number of these trees along the railway line and in the autumn it is possible to have quite a feast on the nuts they drop.

Pass over the stile then follow the edge of the arable field to another stile. Pass over it and through the band of woodland and carry on following the field edge until crossing over the fence via a stile. Go through the gate and past the house, then cross over the road to another stile, pass over it and carry straight on. Cross over the next three stiles. After the third turn right and then, almost immediately, left over another stile onto B 18.

This track is known as Old Wye Lane ▐▐ and was once an important route from Wye to Chartham and then on to Canterbury. Today it has been reduced in some parts to a narrow footpath and others a metalled highway, but this part still retains much of the feel of an ancient green lane. Old Wye Lane is not a place to be at midnight though, as sometimes horses hooves can be heard in the distance; then a ghostly coach drawn by four horses comes silently into view and passes along the lane - allegedly.

At the first cross road of tracks go straight on and at the next cross over onto the Stour Valley Walk. As the path exits the trees turn left and follow the field edge, FP 17, then bear right.

To the left is Julliberrie Down. It is named after a Roman general who local legend states is buried in the large burial mound on the down. The fact behind the legend is that the Roman general Quintus Laberius Durus was killed during the battle at nearby Chilham mentioned earlier, but he was not interned in the grave mound. The grave mound is in fact a Neolithic "A" long barrow and the only representative of its kind in Kent. Many excavations of the barrow have been attempted since the first in 1702 by the Earl of Aylesford and Lord Weymouth. As well as four burials from around the beginning of the Roman occupation artefacts from the Stone, Bronze and Iron Ages have been found.

At the track junction go straight over. Go past the house at the bottom of the slope then turn right over the river.

On the right is Chilham Mill. It is almost certainly on the site of a Saxon mill and is the last survivor of the six mills recorded in the 1085 Domesday Book. The present mill was re-built in the mid-1800s and is considered to be the best preserved of its kind in the south. It is known as a french mill as France was the source of the six pairs of grinding stones that were once operated. It finally ceased production in 1934 and today it houses a pumping station.

Head straight up the road, cross over the level crossing then turn right at the end of the road and retrace the trail back to the railway station.

For details of the village and castle see walk one.

From the Bottom to the Top

2. One for the Tree Lovers

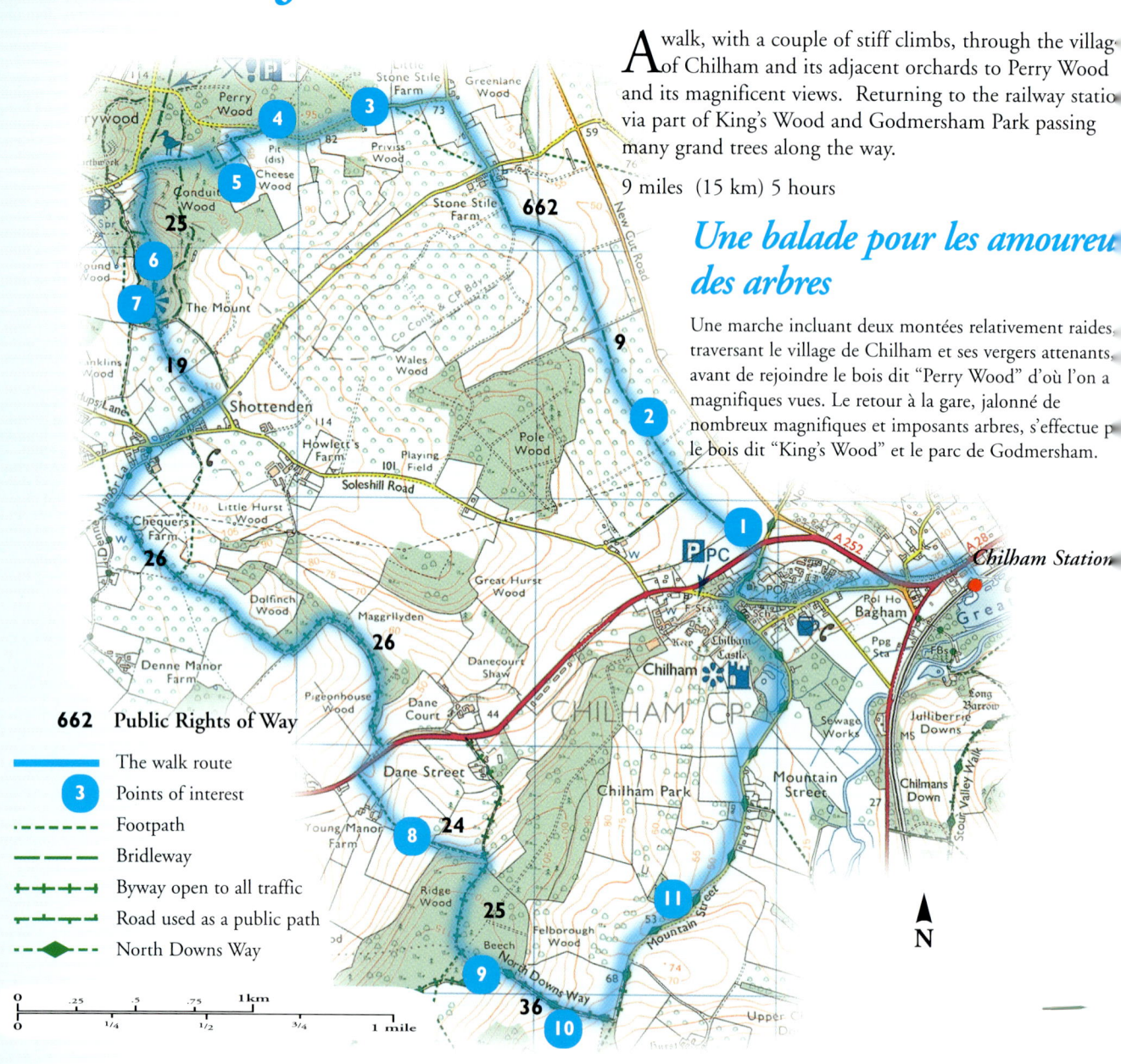

A walk, with a couple of stiff climbs, through the village of Chilham and its adjacent orchards to Perry Wood and its magnificent views. Returning to the railway station via part of King's Wood and Godmersham Park passing many grand trees along the way.

9 miles (15 km) 5 hours

Une balade pour les amoureux des arbres

Une marche incluant deux montées relativement raides, traversant le village de Chilham et ses vergers attenants, avant de rejoindre le bois dit "Perry Wood" d'où l'on a magnifiques vues. Le retour à la gare, jalonné de nombreux magnifiques et imposants arbres, s'effectue p le bois dit "King's Wood" et le parc de Godmersham.

662 Public Rights of Way

— The walk route
3 Points of interest
----- Footpath
— — Bridleway
+−+−+ Byway open to all traffic
−•−•− Road used as a public path
−◆−◆− North Downs Way

10 *One for the Tree Lovers*

From the station follow the route into Chilham as walk one.

For details of the village and castle see walk one.

Leave The Square via Church Hill which is to the left of the White Horse Pub. On reaching the road turn left for a short distance before crossing the road to BW 9 opposite.

In the hedgerow on the left **1** are a number of large elders (Sambucus nigra). Today this very common shrub is most noted for the wine its berries and flowers can be made into, but in the past there was a multitude of folklore attached to it. Its supposed properties were somewhat conflicting: it was viewed as the most evil of trees and one of the most useful. Its bad reputation stems from it supposedly providing the wood for the Cross and being the tree that Judas Iscariot hanged himself from. Many country workers would not burn elder wood as it was thought it caused death and disaster, "raised the Devil" and the fire would show its displeasure by going out. There is some truth in the last part of that statement, as freshly cut elder put onto a bonfire is almost guaranteed to stifle even the most vigorous of blazes. Every part of this inoffensive tree has been considered, at one time or another, to have had malevolent properties.

Pruner at work in a modern apple orchard

Conversely almost every part of it was thought to have beneficial properties. It was thought also to be a cure for almost any illness, from baldness to warts. Strangely, for a tree so capable of invoking the Devil, it was also considered to be one of the best witch deterrents available.

Pass through the gate into the orchard then carry straight on with the wind break to the right.

Although these modern apple orchards **2**, with their dwarfed and short-lived trees, are far removed from the wildlife rich orchards of the past they still have their moments. The mass of pink-tinged blossom produced each spring is a beautiful Kent spectacle and windfall apples in the autumn are a magnet for both resident and migratory thrushes (Turdus sp.). The plentiful supply of discarded apples provides an important re-fuelling source for fieldfares and redwings (Turdus pilaris and T. iliacus) when they arrive for the winter from continental Europe. It is not unusual in late autumn to see hundreds of these thrushes here noisily chattering away as they feast on the fallen fruit.

At the cross road of tracks carry straight on and at the next, but now with the wind break to the left. Head straight on at the next two cross tracks. Follow the track as it bears left, now BW 662, to the metalled road then turn right. On reaching the road cross over and head up the road opposite. At the T-junction turn left.

Beside the road is a hedge **3** containing some typical species of a Kentish hedgerow. They include hawthorn, common dogwood and wayfaring-tree (Crataegus monogyna, Cornus sanguinea and Viburnum lantana). Why wayfaring-tree is so called has been lost in time; it is only one of a number of common wayside shrubs that can be found on this chalky soil. Look out for its creamy-white, lily-scented flowers in early summer or its red, then turning black, berries towards the end of

Wayfaring-tree

One for the Tree Lovers **11**

Ash pollard

summer. When crushed the stems have the disagreeable scent of dogs' urine.

Just after the bend in the road turn left off the road onto BW 25 or continue onwards for refreshment at the Rose and Crown Pub.

Growing beside the first part of the path **4** is woodruff (*Asperula odorata*). It is odourless when fresh but has a sweet hay-like scent with a hint of almond when dried. This made it popular in Tudor houses and churches as an "air-fresherner". It also saw a lot of use in removing musty smells in mattresses, bedding, clothes, wardrobes and library shelves.

As the path passes behind the house **5** there is a wonderful pollarded ash tree (*Fraxinus excelsior*). Judging by the burrs and the hollow trunk it must be many centuries old. Ash was one of the most revered trees in the countryside with uses against witchcraft, in divining the future and as a folk medicine. This reverence stems from the influence the Vikings had on this country's culture around the turn of the first millennium. In Scandinavian mythology Odin fashioned the first man and woman from two ash trunks found on the shore. The branches and roots of Yggdrasil, the word ash tree in Norse mythology, joined together Heaven, Earth and Hell; and after the passing of the old gods a new race of men would arise from its timber.

The path now passes through part of Perry Wood. This wood is owned by Swale Borough Council and today is very popular with walkers, but in the distant past this high ground was the site of a Stone Age encampment. There are earthworks still visible a little further west in the wood. In 1967 excavations found many arrowheads, tools and cooking utensils from that period. It is also thought that invading Roman soldiers took advantage of the great view of the surrounding countryside the site offers by having a camp here.

At the junction of bridleways carry straight on through the gate. After passing through the white gate turn immediately left into the pines. At the top of the slope carry straight on.

As the path clears the trees **6** some far-reaching views can be had. Looking north-east it is possible to see Whitstable and the sea; to the north-west the chimneys of the paper mill at Kemsley, north of Sittingbourne. Even further north it is possible to see the estuary of the River Medway and the chimney of Kingsnorth power station on the Isle of Grain. A little further along the path is a wooden viewing platform **7** . This replaced an older structure known as the Pulpit. There is a belief that it was built for preachers to use but it is more likely that it was constructed by one of the Earls of Sondes so he could survey his estates from this excellent view point. Again, the views of the surrounding countryside are superb; looking east Canterbury Cathedral can be seen and, on a clear day, the sea at Pegwell Bay.

Carry straight on down the steps. Pass straight over the cross-road of tracks to a stile. Pass over the stile and follow FP 19, through the orchard keeping the fence to the right. As the fence ends bear left and then right and over the stile onto the road. Turn right and follow the road into the hamlet of Shottenden.

The meaning of the name of this hamlet is a reference to

North from the Pulpit

12 *One for the Tree Lovers*

the high ground it lies at the foot of. It has evolved from the Old English scëoting dün meaning a shooting or projecting hill. During the Second World War a shell from the German gun "Big Bertha" firing from Calais hit the village. Allegedly the explosion blew off two of a gypsy's fingers, on one of which was the ring of the King of the Gypsies. Despite a frantic search by all the gypsies from near and far it was never found.

Bear right at the T-junction then turn left at the cross-roads. At the T-junction turn left onto B 26. Follow the long track to the road. Cross over the road and turn right along the footpath until turning left to Young Manor Farm. As the track bears right carry straight on over the stile, FP 24. Head diagonally right across the field to the fence, then bear left and follow the fence.

Around the ruins at the bottom of the bank and up the side of the field are some huge sycamore trees (Acer pseudoplatanus) **8**. This fifteenth or sixteenth century addition from central Europe to this country's flora is viewed by some as a pest as it is very adept at establishing itself, sometimes at the expense of native wildlife. But, when allowed to grow as large as these mighty trees, it can

Sycamore bark

become a striking feature of any landscape. In the relatively short space of time this tree has been on these shores it has already acquired its share of folk law. In the west of the country there is a tradition of baking buns or pastries on sycamore leaves so that they have an imprint of the leaf on their undersides; this may be a continuation of the belief that this tree is useful in deterring the attentions of fairies.

Follow the fence line to and cross the stile on the left of the wood. The path carries on in the same direction until it reaches a track. Turn right along this track, BW 25.

The trail now passes through Ridge Wood which is part of the King's Wood complex. This part of King's Wood contains some of its oldest trees. The path passes a number of majestic beech trees (Fagus sylvatica) **9**. There is some debate as to whether beech is a true native or a Roman introduction to this country. The controversy is fuelled by the fact that it does seem to struggle in some of its haunts. The summer droughts of the last few years have seen many large beeches showing signs of stress and it is very prone to being thrown in high winds - as was evidenced in the 1987 hurricane. But beech pollen dating from 6000 BC has been found in Hampshire. As this pre-dates the opening of the Channel by 500 years it means beech just passes the test set by botanists for being a true native - it was here before Britain became an island.

When the North Downs Way comes in from the right carry straight on, now BW 36.

To the right is Godmersham Park. For details of the estate see walk two. The bank **10** that runs down the right-hand side of the path was constructed by one of the previous owners of the estate to prevent people using this right of way from having a view of the house, although it is possible to get glimpses of the building through gaps in the bank.

At the bottom of the slope turn left and follow the path. After a short distance it leads onto a road, carry on in the same direction.

Along the left-hand side of the road **11** are fine examples of another species of tree; this time horse chestnuts (Aesculus hippocastanum). This well-known source of conkers is now considered an "honorary native" tree, but is truly native to the Balkans. The seed was brought to northern Europe from Constantinople by the botanist Charles de l'Ecluse in 1576. The derivation of the name is not really known. In its native Turkey it is given to horses both as food and medicine. Also when a leaf falls off, it leaves behind a horseshoe-shaped scar complete with nail-like marks. Perhaps because of its more southerly origins, it is one of the first large trees to come into leaf in the spring, and the first to turn brown as autumn approaches.

Follow the road back to The Square at Chilham and retrace the route back to the railway station.

Beech in Ridge Wood

One for the Tree Lovers **13**

3. Around the Lake

A gentle walk around Chilham Lake. Although short the walk offers plenty of opportunity to experience a host of wetland wildlife at this peaceful spot. Access is by permission of Mid-Kent Water.

1.5 miles (2 km) 1 hour

Autour du lac

Une marche accessible à tous autour du lac de Chilham. Bien qu'étant courte, cette balade offre de nombreuses opportunités de se familiariser en ce coin tranquille avec toute une foule de plantes et d'animaux caractéristiques des milieux humides.

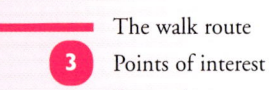

Public Rights of Way
- The walk route
- 3 Points of interest
- Footpath
- Bridleway
- Byway open to all traffic
- Road used as a public path

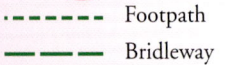

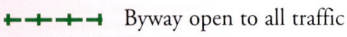

14 *Around the Lake*

From the station go to the main road and turn left. Keep left at the next junction then a little further turn left down the road sign-posted Chilham Mill then cross over the railway.

On the left is a stand of trees **1** comprised mostly of ash and hybrid black poplars (Fraxinus excelsior and Populus nigra var. betulifolia). These fairly characterless poplars are a far cry from the trees of their origin. A true black poplar is much more interesting with a deeply fissured trunk covered in bosses and burrs, growing up to 30 metres (100 feet) and often having a pronounced lean by the time the tree is middle-aged. What was once a common river-side tree is now a scarce sight, with perhaps fewer than five thousand remaining. Examples appear in a number of John Constable's landscapes painted in a different Stour Valley in Suffolk, including his most well-known work The Hay Wain (1821) - which itself may have been planked with black poplar timber.

These trees are good for spotted flycatchers (Muscicapa strriata); from early summer until they leave for Africa in the autumn. They nest in a tree fork or in one of the nest-boxes provided. Listen out for their almost mouse-like squeaks from the trees or look out for one as it

Chilham Lake

springs from the end of a branch to snatch an nsect, very often repeatedly returning to the same perch.

Just before reaching the river turn left along the path beside it.

Chilham Lake is one of a number of disused gravel pits in this part of the Stour Valley. Today it is managed as a fishing lake by Mid-Kent Water and the management of the lake is largely sympathetic to its wildlife.

Views across the lake are available from the fishing platforms beside the path. It is a good spot for seeing water-fowl and one bird normally present all year is great-crested grebe (Podiceps cristatus). These days it is almost guaranteed that this colourful bird can be found on any expanse of open water, but less than a century ago it was one of this country's rarest birds. Its feathers were a prized material for decorating hats and it was virtually hunted to extinction to supply this trade. Its plight prompted the formation of an organisation that developed into the Royal Society for the Protection of Birds (RSPB). Their first success was saving the last few pairs of grebe in Norfolk and they have since gone from strength to strength. Perhaps the RSPB should have the great-crested grebe as its logo instead of the avocet (Recurvirostra avosetta).

Growing in the shallow margins of the lake are stands of yellow iris (Iris pseudocorus). Iris in a river reveals its shallowness and maybe the presence of a ford. In the fifth century the king of the Franks, Clovis led his out-numbered Merovingian army to safety from the Goths across a ford so marked on the Rhine. He adopted the iris as his badge and it is possible that the French fleur de lys originated from that event.

The bank-side of the lake **2** is home to many familiar water-side plants. They include gipsywort, water mint and hemlock water dropwort (Lycopus europaeus, Mentha aquatica and Oenanthe crocata). One very noticeable plant with its tall spikes of purple flowers towards the end of summer is purple-loosestrife (Lythrum salicaria). The name refers to the ancient belief that if a sprig of this plant was placed on the yoke of a pair of inharmonious oxen it would stop their

Great-crested grebes

Around the Lake **15**

Purple-loosestrife

quarrelling. Purple-loosestrife was used by John Everett Millais in his 1851 painting of Ophelia drowning, to depict the "long purples" of Shakespeare's description of her death garland (Hamlet IV. vii), although it was more likely that he had early-purple orchids (Orchis mascula) in mind.

On reaching the metal gate turn left and continue on around the lake.

The water-side **3** is also populated by a number of wetland trees. Some such as alder (Alnus glutinosa) are fairly easy to identify, but others such as the various willows (Salix spp.) are a little more challenging. Three similar looking willows that grow here are white, crack and osier (Salix alba, fragilis and viminalis). All three have similar long leaves but crack willow leaves do not have the glaucous undersides of the other two. Both crack and white willow tend to be large trees whereas osier is a much smaller, multi-stemmed shrub. To make things even more difficult they all hybridise with each other, so there is the possibility of plants exhibiting combinations of the characteristics of all three.

One member of the willow family that is much easier to identify is white poplar (Populus alba) with its leaves coated with a white down on their undersides, from a distance giving the tree the appearance of being covered in snow. Its origins are not entirely known. It was first thought to have been a seventeenth century introduction from southern Europe, but there are many references to it under its old name, "abel", in thirteenth century documents. So it must either have been introduced much earlier or is a true native to these shores.

Scrambling through the hedge **4** on the right of the path are a number of dog roses (Rosa canina). Once the pink-tinged white flowers have "gone over" they are replaced by the familiar bright red rose-hips. It was noted in the 1930s that wild rose-hips contain a higher proportion of vitamin C than any other common fruit or vegetable; a cup of rose-hip pulp has more vitamin C than forty oranges. This fact played a part in this country's war effort during the Second World War. In 1941, with the usual sources (citrus fruit) of that important vitamin badly disrupted, the Government instigated a scheme for the collection of rose-hips that were then made into rose-hip syrup. In its first year one hundred and twenty tons were collected and this had risen to over four hundred and fifty tons by the time the war ended. Children played a major part in the success, with whole schools taking part in collecting expeditions in late summer. With 3d (1.5 pence) a pound being paid to collectors, budding entrepreneurs could earn much more than just pocket money.

On reaching the road re-trace the way back to the station.

Child picking rose-hips

16 *Around the Lake*

4. The Down Walk

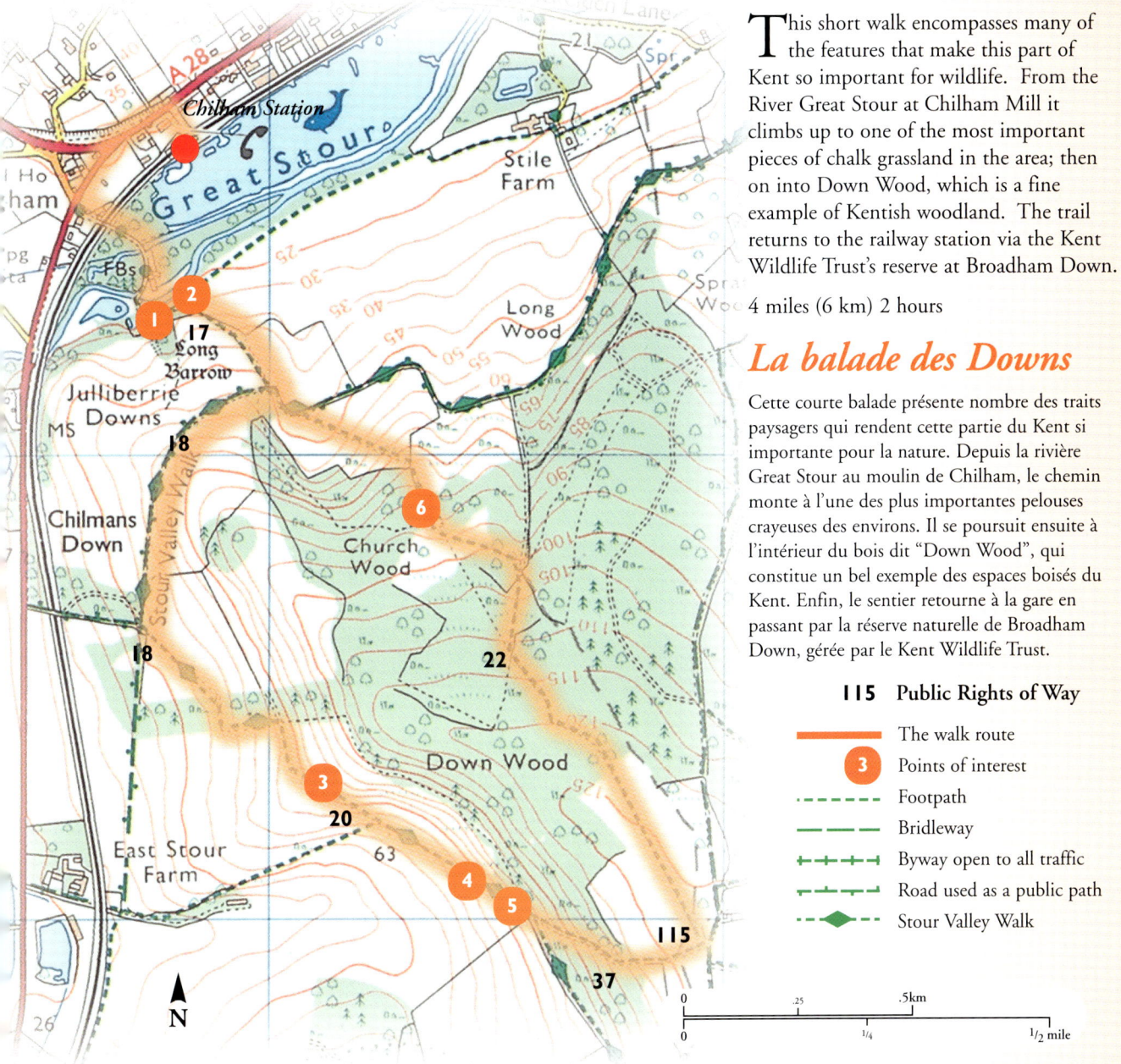

This short walk encompasses many of the features that make this part of Kent so important for wildlife. From the River Great Stour at Chilham Mill it climbs up to one of the most important pieces of chalk grassland in the area; then on into Down Wood, which is a fine example of Kentish woodland. The trail returns to the railway station via the Kent Wildlife Trust's reserve at Broadham Down.

4 miles (6 km) 2 hours

La balade des Downs

Cette courte balade présente nombre des traits paysagers qui rendent cette partie du Kent si importante pour la nature. Depuis la rivière Great Stour au moulin de Chilham, le chemin monte à l'une des plus importantes pelouses crayeuses des environs. Il se poursuit ensuite à l'intérieur du bois dit "Down Wood", qui constitue un bel exemple des espaces boisés du Kent. Enfin, le sentier retourne à la gare en passant par la réserve naturelle de Broadham Down, gérée par le Kent Wildlife Trust.

Symbol	Description
115	Public Rights of Way
—	The walk route
3	Points of interest
- - -	Footpath
– –	Bridleway
+++	Byway open to all traffic
++++	Road used as a public path
- ◆ -	Stour Valley Walk

Stewards of the Countryside **17**

Follow the same route to Chilham Mill as walk three. Where the path turns off to Chilham lake carry straight on over the river towards Chilham Mill.

For details of the mill see walk one.

Cross over the next bridge and follow the path as it bears left, FP 17.

The bridge **1** is a good spot for grey wagtail (Motacilla cinerea). This colourful bird is scarce in Lowland Britain, preferring fast flowing streams further north. But here, where the mill race produces the highly oxygenated water conditions that the wagtails' insect prey require, it is possible to see one or two of these birds. Each summer they nest under or close to one of the bridges.

Growing in abundance on either side of the path **2** is hart's-tongue fern (Phyllitis scolopendrium). This evergreen fern is the only one in North West Europe that has undivided leaves making identification easy.

At the junction of paths carry straight on.

On the right is Julliberrie Down. For details of this burial mound see page nine.

When the path meets the broad track turn right, BW 18.

Gaps in the hedge on the right allow views of Chilham Castle - for details of the castle see walk one.

At the cross road of tracks turn left, FP 20. Cross diagonally right over the field, heading for the middle of the band on trees. Pass through the trees and turn left to follow the woodland edge. Pass through the next band of trees and then turn right along the woodland edge.

This field is managed as a traditional hayfield **3**. As no artificial fertilisers or pesticides are used on it and the hay is cut late in the summer it is rich in wildlife. It has many nectar rich flowers which, in high summer, are very attractive to butterflies. On hot days from the end of June right through until August clouds of meadow browns, gatekeepers and marbled whites (Maniola jurtina, Pyronia tithonus and Melanargia galathea) can be found.

Marbled white butterfly on black knapweed

Another noticeable plant in this field, especially around the entrance, is chicory (Cichorium intybus). This blue member of the daisy family is native to this type of grassland but is never very abundant. It is a cultivated variety of this plant that is grown as a salad vegetable and its dried and ground-up roots have long been used as an additive to coffee.

Mid-way along the hedge cross diagonally left to a stile through another hedge.

The small field ahead, Down Wood Bank **4**, is one of the most important pieces of chalk grassland in Kent. Not only is it full of many common species of plant associated with this habitat, it has its share of rarities too. Two nationally scarce plants,

Hart's tongue fern

18 *The Down Walk*

Pyramidal orchid

small bedstraw and man orchid (Galium pumilum and Aceras anthropophorum) can be found here. The orchid colony is one of the biggest in the county. Although not the most colourful of orchids their sheer abundance makes them un-missable towards the end of June. The flower that makes the greatest visual impact on the site is pyramidal orchid (Anacamptis pyramidalis), great swathes of the bank can be coated purple with them. Careful searching can also produce a few of this country's most colourful orchids - bee orchid (Ophrys apifera). The shape of the flower is thought to have originally evolved to trick bees into attempting to mate with it, helping with pollen transfer. This has never been reliably observed and in this country the flowers are self pollinating.

The bank's importance for wildlife has been known for a long time. It was notified as a Site of Special Scientific Interest (SSSI) in 1990 and since the mid-1990s it has undergone extensive restoration, with most of the work being undertaken by volunteers from the Kentish Stour Countryside Project. The work has entailed fencing the site so it can be grazed and the clearance of a large proportion of the scrub that had begun to invade. After a great deal of hard work the bank is now managed on a "care and maintenance" basis with a third of site cut each year to keep the regenerating scrub in check until such time as the grazing takes that job over.

Follow the path to the right down the bank. At the bottom follow the fence to a stile. Cross over the stile and turn left.

The scrub clearance programme at Down Wood Bank has had to be tempered for species that benefit from scrub. Each summer the scrub that the path **5** now passes through contains two or three pairs of nightingale (Luscinia megarhynchos) and yellowhammers (Emberiza citrinella) nest in the bushes on the bank. The site is also important for adders (Vipera berus) which like to hide up in the shade created by the scrub when the day becomes too hot for them. Wildlife conservation is never straight forward, all the species of a site have to be considered in its management, not just the rare ones, and any works carried out must be tailored so that the bio-diversity of the area is not adversely affected.

Lady orchid

Cattle grazing, following the fencing of Down Wood Bank

The Down Walk **19**

Broadham Down

At the cross road of paths carry straight on, FP 37 then FP 115. Pass over the stile and continue straight on. After a short distance turn left back across the field, FP 93 then FP 22. Cross over two stiles and enter the wood.

This is Down Wood and is part of the complex known as Denge Wood. This part of the complex is one of the most wildlife rich areas and is a SSSI. It contains a number of woodland orchids including lady orchid and broad-leaved helleborine (Orchis purpurea and Epipactis helleborine). The lady orchids can be found in huge numbers, and because of this it is easy to forget that it is one of the rarest wildflowers in the country. It only occurs in these calcareous woods on the North Downs in Kent as it is very much on the northern edge of its range in Europe.

A close look at the flower will reveal why this gorgeous orchid is so called - each floret looks like a woman in a crinoline ball-gown. Its relative abundance in this county, although recent times has seen a decline, saw it being sold as a cut flower on street corners, even as late as the 1940s.

At the Y-junction of paths bear left. The path passes through a rambler gate and continues down the side of a recently cleared piece of grassland.

The chalk grassland on the right is Broadham Down **6** and was donated to the Kent Wildlife Trust (KWT) in 1997. When it was acquired by KWT it was covered in dense scrub, it is now undergoing the same transformation as Down Wood Bank, for almost the same reasons, and its continuing careful management will in time restore it to the same high quality. Again the vast majority of the work was carried out by volunteers.

Follow the fence line and pass through another rambler gate. Pass through an area of scrub and cross diagonally left over the field to the track then turn left, BW 18. After a short distance turn right and then retrace the route back to the station.

Volunteers from the Kentish Stour Countryside Project fencing at Down Wood Bank

20 *The Down Walk*